Thoughts from the Journey Through

Bill DeRoche

Published by
The Wordshed
Duluth, Minnesota

ISBN: 0-942684-25-7

Arrow Printing
Bemidji, Minnesota

How did I come to write poetry?

In the third grade a teacher sent me to a summer poetry class at the College of St. Scholastica. It was the first time anyone said to me I could do something, and it started me on a journey.

When I finally started writing poetry, I was in high school. For years I hid my writings for fear they would be destroyed by my father and oldest brother.

Today, looking back, I can thank them for giving me the time to work on my art, and the time to let the art grow within me. It's truly been a journey through the last frontier—the journey through the mind.

Hence the title of the book:
Thoughts from the Journey Through.

Bill DeRoche
Knife River, Minnesota
Spring, 2004

Copies of this book may be obtained from:
The Poetry Shed
P.O. Box 225, Knife River, MN 55609

Acknowledgements

Dale and Sally Rogers
who said I should publish my poetry.

Rev. Lloyd and Elsie Mattson
for their encouragement and direction.

Kevin Mattson
for layout and typesetting.

David DeRoche and Terry and Sook DeRoche
for moral support and contributing to the
publication costs.

Tom and Natalie Bothwell
for friendship and encouragement.

Richard Sheehan
for keeping the poetry safe for 20 years, until I gained
confidence to know I had something to say.

John and Marilynn Kessler
and to all who inspired me over the years, in personal
and practical ways.

Mary McHardy
wrote the music and sings my Lake Superior poem.
My heart skips a beat every time I hear it.
Thanks, Mary.

Photo Credit

To Travis Melin
Thanks, my friend. May your journey to photograph
nature's beauty fulfill your life.

Letters

A letter from one of Bill's teachers:

Dear Bill,

I'm leaving Duluth rather abruptly, so I won't get a chance to give you these [poems] in person. I truly enjoyed them and praised God for gracing you with talent, and for you, that you are putting his gifts to creative use.

I'm heading for Florida—may or may not remain there in new ministry. I'm searching. In any case, it will be East and as far South as possible! I'm torn between "roots and wings!"

Our Lord and Lady be your best friends unto eternity, Bill!

Your old teacher,
Sister Jeanne Moran

A letter from a former teacher at North Hennepin Community College, Brooklyn Park, MN

Bill DeRoche   February 22, 2000
Knife River, MN

Dear Bill:

I hope this packet turns out to be a pleasant surprise for you.

Recently, our English office got relocated to another building as a result of a major renovation project. This meant that we had to pack up all our files and books and then unpack them again in the new facility.

At the bottom of one of my file drawers was a plain, brown envelope marked "Bill DeRoche." It was in the bunch of things that I had not looked at in about 20 years. The name rang a bell, because I frequently remember the names of students from even 30 or 35 years ago. I also save all of the class lists going back to 1965. I recalled the name from the late 1970's and so I located your name in a Fall Quarter, 1978 class list.

I also remembered you telling me that you were from the Duluth-North Shore area. I recall having several interesting chats with you about the North Shore. In the library I found a Duluth phone book and looked you up. There you were—living in Knife River.

I must have hung onto your poetry for several quarters, expecting that you would re-enroll some time and then stop by my office to pick it up. That's probably how it got put in the bottom file drawer—waiting, waiting, waiting, but in a safe place. I'm guessing that's how I forgot about it for all of these years.

Bill, I'm very sorry that your excellent poetry sat in that drawer for all of these years. I re-read all of it yesterday and I like it very much. It has beauty and honest sentiment. I particularly like the one entitled "Blooming."

I've sent this packet by certified mail so that there is no danger of it getting lost. If you would like to drop me a note, I've put a stamped, self-addressed envelope in with this letter. I'd like to hear from you.

Sincerely,
Richard Sheehan

Duluth News Tribune Article, "Lake Effect"
July 28, 2002

In 1967, Bill DeRoche decided to return to his hometown of Duluth from Long Island, NY, after his wife and baby died in childbirth.

"I came back so depressed I thought of committing suicide," he said.

DeRoche planned to swim out into Lake Superior until he could no longer swim, then let the lake take him under.

While driving on US Highway 53 through Superior, he turned off at Connors Point and made his way to the shore of Superior Bay.

"The minute I saw the water, I cried myself to sleep on the shore," he said.

When he woke, he discovered someone had covered him with a wool blanket and left a thermos of coffee and a lunch box with a peanut butter and jam sandwich. There also was a note that said, "The lake will heal you."

It was the beginning of a process of healing for him that took several years. Out of his experience, he wrote a poem called "Lake Superior, My Lake of Life." The poem talks about what the moods of the lake have taught him, all the while "ever giving and never asking."

It took him 12 years to get the poem just the way he wanted it—to say to the world what the lake means to him.

Now 62, he is retired and lives in Knife River. He often walks up the shoreline of the lake. Sometimes he drives up the North Shore and meets people and tells them about his poetry about Lake Superior. He sells copies of his poems sometimes, but he often winds up giving them away—wanting to share his love for life and the lake.

Story by Linda Hanson

Part One

~Lake Effect~

Lake Superior
(My Lake of Life)

My lake of life
That gives the blue
To the heaven's eye

The emerald green
That spreads every outward
To give life its dreams

Its white caps that move
Ever onward
And tell me I cannot
Stand still

The icy blue stare
That beckons me to look
Ever deeper in life

Its thunderous roar that
Lends itself
To the applause for life

My lake of life
Ever giving and
Never asking

The place of refuge
In the time of
Turmoil

Its shimmering sun's reflection
To help us dance
For joy

The day of calm
That gives life its rest
To renew one's quest for life

My lake of life
Ever giving and
Never asking

The shroud covered days
That renew the
Mysteries of life

Its gloomy mournful days
That give time to remember
Those who have gone

Storm tossed anger days
To teach us to clear
The anger from our souls

Moonbeams upon the water
That calm the spirit
And bring forth love

Ever giving and
Never asking
My lake of life

For someone unknown, who is full of wisdom.

The Beach

I walk the beach
of today
A beach of memories

With no one there

The footprints of today
fall upon the prints
of many yesterdays

They both disturb
and comfort
the heart

For the beach
is lonely
Yet full of love

For life is always
two of one

For Gary and Cami Krutke,
because walking the beach makes good friends.

Inland Sea

If I but may sail
forever and a day
the Inland Sea

Then my being set free
shall remain free
forever and a day
sailing the Inland Sea

For I find my strength
for being
my hope
for being
the love of giving
and receiving
sailing the Inland Sea

My tattered course
upon the land
the compass with no pints
all find themselves
set right
when I set sail
on the Inland Sea

*For Norm and Mae Livgard,
for sharing a journey to the Apostle Islands*

Life in the Waves

The waves that began
with time
And will only end
at the end of the
eons of time

One by one the waves
come rolling in
Sometimes one at a
time
Often in tempest
ten on ten

Through the sun-filled days
the waves come in
In tempest they swell
to frighten even
the brave

More often than not
the waves come in
Filling your head with
a sound
Paralleled by no other

Walking and listening
to the waves come in
Gives time to pause,
to pause and listen to the
waves come in

The Blue Lake

To the lake my spirit must go

To the blue lake my spirit must go

To dance from whitecap to whitecap

To the blue lake my spirit must go

To the arms every beckoning
that give the spirit its freedom

To the blue lake my spirit must go

To where all cares are diminished
and the spirit can soar

To the blue lake my spirit must go

To a new baptism into life

To the blue lake I must go

To grow to the child within

Bill,   *March 11, 1973*

*Thank you for a beautifully mellow weekend. Your love
and compassion surpasses your creativity in mind. Always
remember me as one who is sitting on the edge of tomorrow,
listing to the love grow.*

A brief moment of eternity,
Peace always,
Bob Overturf

Friendship

If friends could be counted
as numerous as stones on the beach
how rich we would be
But the stones know not we

How fortunate we are
when good friends
can be counted to three
One in particular is polished
to shine for thee
He in particular knows
the troubled side of your soul
and still cares to walk with thee

You give and take
but forever the bond is true
You've learned to share
the joys and sorrows
that make your lives grow

The years come
and the years go
You learn to speak
in the silence of your souls

The days come when thoughts
turn to memories
And rekindle the love
of friendship

Time gives way
to the passing of time
And death beguiled
when love of friendship
leads the way

The Gales of November

And so begins
the gales of November

The lake takes on a mournful
blue
or a vengeful
hue

The wind in participation
turns icy cold and
blows with vengeance

Together they raise waves
that give man pause
to think
That one should not sail
in the gales of November

One sets forth and holds
your spirit in reserve
The day is bright and sunny
when from nowhere comes
the black clouds, the wind
and so begins
the gales of November

All is within
perseverance is what wins
not the faint-heated

Storm tossed waves know not
who they buffet, the wind,
this is my month
to blow and blow
The roar is deafening, is it
they who have gone before
"Do not sail in
the gales of November"

Push on, push on
do not listen
Life is meant to be lived
Push on, push on
do not fret
the gales of November

We can overcome,
all is within
perseverance is what wins
not the faint hearted

Yet one does pause
to listen to
the gales of November

For all who sail the Inland Sea

17

Lighthouses

From the fog of
distant time
Shines the point
of light

That at one time
brought ships home
To safe harbor for
family, home
and friends

The turning of the light
at the Two Harbors light
keeps alive the history
of lighthouses

Telling marines
this is your safe home
When the inland sea
fills you with fright

Others live on in
the history of man
Fine sentinels
That give warmth
to the heart

In a trip back in time

Need

Between the edge of
the sand
and the edge of
the water

Lies the sound of
yesterday
today
and tomorrow

Listen, it has its need
as you have
yours,
In the time of need
its own answer
to the need

Song of the Lake

Sing to me gently
Sing to me often
Sing to me the song
most often forgotten

The song of the wave that
embraces the shore

Every river and stream
sings the song of joy

Trees in their whispering
sing, I am here for you

Islands of beauty that
sing rest with me

In the vastness of blue the
song, come play with me

In the time of forevering
the lake sings to all
a gentle
love
song

Listening Point

I go to the lake
to listen

Nothing more
to listen

Of the ages I haven't lived
to listen
To the age to which I live
to listen
To the ages yet to come
(as their whisper begins)
to listen

In the listening I find myself
becalmed
to the listening

I become one to all the ages
listen
I am and I am not

For Mary and Paul
who truly listen

Seasons of the Witch's Tree

Kindred Spirits of
ages gone by
ages to come
Fill the time of the
Witch's Tree

A day marked only one
in the time of the
Witch's Tree

Not so marked
by the Witch's Tree

The seasons come
the seasons go

Marked only by the rings
of the Witch's Tree

All who come in the
seasons of the
Witch's Tree
Yearn to come again in the
Seasons of the Witch's Tree

Thoughts from
the Journey Through

~Listening and Thinking~

Listening and Thinking

I emptied my head
upon the table near
to see what was there

I sorted through
some things I kept
some things I threw
some things I set
aside to think anew

I thought as I
sorted through
No wonder you take
such a narrow view
your mind's been clogged
with no room to
think anew

It took time
but the time
was well spent

For I have an
open mind
with which to spend
a lot of time

Listening and thinking
to all minds

The Last Frontier

I wish you well
on your journey through
the last frontier

The journey of many roads,
of mountains, valleys,
rainbows and downpours

Side trips of not
lost time
but of adventures
that broaden
the journey

Of time in waiting
that is not lost
but renews the spirit
to continue the journey

This journey sometimes done
with great strides
often times done
an inch at a time

I wish you well
in your journey through
the last frontier

The journey through
the mind

Blooming

The thistle bush
grows so all alone
So tall and straight
in a beautiful
green

Yet who would dare
touch
For its thorny leaves

But once a year
it blooms
In a most beautiful flower
as soft as silk

And beckons all
to come and touch
For I too am in need
of love and you

So in patience
I wait
For the thistle bush
to bloom

Just as I wait and watch
for you
In the hope that once
a year
You will bloom and
lay aside
your thorns that say
do not touch

And bring forth
a flower
That will say
I, too, am in need
of love
Please come
and touch

My teacher, Richard Sheehan's favorite

Ramblings

In time of ramblings
I speak

I speak softly and in their
ramblings they do not hear

I speak softly of love, as love
is tendering of the heart

I live in love as life is meant
to be in love

I search to give of my all
and I wait

I hear your ramblings
and I wait
for you to speak

Thoughts

Here I sit thinking thoughts
of you
Thinking thoughts how
great and true
And now I've met you
and I found that you are you

Who's Wise?

A turtle is slow
but awfully wise

He taught the hare
what man
will never know

His time is long
and yet he knows
That time is his
to loose as he chooses

For no one yet
in their time
Has taught the turtle
to hurry his
own time

The Sum

The sum of who I am
is also
the sum of whom
I chose
not to be

Words

Better it be to give forth
with words true
Than forever in silence
to be subdued

For one word uttered out
Could be the breath
for a soul renewed

For a life astrew a regathering
of all that was ever
in a life anew

Think

If the wars we fight
with ourselves

Are battles that
we win

There would be no time
for wars
That engulf our
fellow men

And hasten our
precious earth
to its bitter end

The Wind

The wind whispers
the mind remembers
and life goes on

Endure

To stare into the depths
of a star lit heavenly
night

To see the first flame
of the growing morning
sun

To bask in the heat of day
and see the glory of things
grow

To catch the brilliance of the
setting sun that mingles the
day with the night

With the glory of these
happenings each day

Instills in each man the
power to endure

Passion

I'd much rather
have lived
a life
of passion

Than lived
a life
of passion
for longevity

A Point of Being

I do not know who I am
I only know I am being

And in my being, will give me
time to know who I am

For life is
a point of being

Against Discrimination

To be
To let be
To help be
All that we can be

The Journey

The journey is not
over
The journey yet
to come
Is the journey that beckons
us all to become
One

Thoughts from
the Journey Through

~Precious Gifts~

Precious Gifts

My child these gifts
I give to you

The most precious gifts
I've found
I wish to share
with you

Love
Anger

Peace
Tempest

Solitude
Togetherness

For to give only half
of these

Is to share only half of
what I've found

And that would be
no gift of sharing

I give these to you
in equal measure

That you may know
how to put your
life together

For to know one
without the other

Is to know
nothing at all

Hope

I have no
Hope
For the world as a
whole

But I have
all the Hope
in the universe
for many of the
individuals
in it

Please be
one of the many
individuals in it

For Sally Rogers, who is one
of the individuals in it

Night

In the breath of time
I've discovered
night

In my solitude
the wonderment of
night

No moon to shadow make
No lines drawn in the
night

No stars to limit the
night

Endless space, endless space in the
night

All fears thrown out in the
night

I am me, I am me in the dark of
night

Color no difference makes to the
night

The mirror no reflection, no guilt
in the night

Laughter at myself in hindsight
in the night

Tears may fall for love or lack of
in the night

I am me in the dark
of night

Just One Heart

Is there a heart like mine
one that hurts and loves like mine

Is there a heart like mine
one that loves to live like mine
One that changes like the tide
One that wanders through the
open countryside

Is there a heart like mine
one that yearns for the simple
things
One that will ring with all the
joy it sings

Is there a heart like mine

Time

Take a second, make it an hour
Time?
Take a minute and make it a day
Time?
Take a day and make it a year
Time?

Time is only measured by the
here and now
The mind is forever and knows not
measured time
My mind waits to share with you
here and now
Take the time, the time
to share

The Mask

Too long O love
have you been denied

Covered by a mask
that was presented by a lie

Denied by a laugh
built by a mask

Now is the time
to pause

To pause and destroy
the mask

To give demise
to a lie

And let it be for you
to judge

To judge and decide
if we have loved

Mr. Tin Man

Mr. tin man can you loan me a dime
I am so far away from home
and haven't a dime to dine

Mr. Tin man you've spent your time
to earn your dime
The centuries have taught
you the dime is fine
and now your time is spent
and what is the worth of your dime

My time has taught me the
mind is fine
I have my time to spend,
but not in search of a dime
I search in you to find that which is fine

Betwixt

Betwixt the time that I've
been born and the time I must die
May I come to know just
two souls
Yours and mine

For mine is a must
for me to know
That I might share it
with those I know

Yours is for you to know
So you can share it with
whom you know

We have no light to share
unless we know the soul
Though we have things to share
without the light
I care not to share
without the light

You

Though you have gone
you make the world bright

I see your face in the
rising sun
Your smile in the ripples
of the water
Your eyes in the blue
of the Day

Though you have gone
you make the world bright

I go on in a smile
and calm,
With a light hearted walk
With love in my heart
for all that I meet

Though you have gone
you make the world bright

To that someone special I walked only a mile with

To Know

There is a soul that
I know
And I wonder if it
is really mine

For I find that it
is very often
a stranger unto me

At times it gives me
great comfort
to know this strange
soul

And other times it tears
the marrow of my bones
for the want of an answer
to whom it belongs

Though I search
each day
to know the whole
of this soul

It remains a life long
challenge to know
the wonderment
of this strange soul

Father
(On His Death)

He never said hello
I never said goodbye

Does that leave us wanting
in each other's eyes

One waited
one ignored

What then of time
in between
lost or stolen

Dreams, Dreams of,
left to Dream

The ache of love
left to ache

He never said hello
I never said goodbye

All That Heaven Allows

Let all the heavens resound
for I love
I've bent my knee
and loved the sapling
Have brushed the feathers
of the wild abode
Out stretched my arms
and absorbed love

Let all the heavens resound
for I love

I've touched your hand
and felt my heart aglow
Searched your eyes
and seen forever
Caressed your smile and now know
love is forever

Time's End
(Epitaph for Bill)

The sun is setting
after so many risings

Moon is full
one more time

The time of my hellos
has become the time
of my goodbyes

My eyes rest gently
on those who said hello
I take that with me
into the corridors of time

I leave behind, that which
I can take with me

Love that knows no bounds

Thoughts from
the Journey Through

~Wings of Understanding~

"The wings of understanding protect the flame of intellect"

The drawing that inspired a poem that inspired a carving.

Frank Hill, friend and artist wood carver, gave me the drawing to use in this book. The drawing inspired my descriptive poem. I returned both to Frank who created a wonderful carving to express his idea and my words in walnut and mahogany.

The carving (pictured on the back cover of this book) and poem now hang at Northwood's Children's Services in Duluth.

Sea of Faces

If I could but stay
for awhile
How my heart would
like to share a day
with you

But my mind races
on
And tells that this day
is not mine

For I see a sea of
faces
And know that your time
is not mine

Maybe in time
you will come to know
How my heart has waited
to spend a day
with you

I can but only search
this sea of faces
And some day hope
to meet you
in the sea of faces

Dreamer

If I but be a dreamer
then proudly dream
shall I

Of seas yet to sail
of stars yet to see

Of these I dream
proudly dream
shall I

The days spent making
chariots out of clouds
a magic carpet of a leaf
upon the wind

Of these I dream
proudly dream
shall I

Laying on a hillside dreaming
of love for the world round
to enfold that love
through eternity

Of these I dream
proudly dream
shall I

The child in me is
the dreamer
the man in me giving
vent to the child

Of these I dream
proudly dream
shall I

Come join me in a day
of dreaming
Let your dreams give
you wings

If I but be a dreamer
then proudly dream
shall I

The Hour

'Tis not I that should judge
you by the hour

'Tis not for you to judge yourself
by the hour, so that you do
not recognize the hour

To each is given their hour
to shine
A life time to live
to shine
for just one hour

Then live your life as
you may
Be aware that soon
the hours
will number down to one
and yet
that too may be your
shining
hour

To the Two of You

To the two of you too dear
for me to know
To the two of you too wise for
me to know
To the two of you with hearts
of love known

To the two of you surrounded
by years of joy
To the two of you in embering
years glistening
To the two of you with
memories unfurled

To the two of you in child's
eyes agleam
To the two of you in God's
memory supreme

To the two of you to dear for
me to know

On my grandparents' 60th wedding anniversary.

Our Union

If there could be a way
to stop all time
and forever hold this day
as yours and mine

I would gladly give
all the days I have
for this one day
to have with you

For no other time
is so great
as the first day
of our lives

Our union
has been chosen
by the two
of us

And is the fulfillment
of a dream
of someone to love
who loves me

What is Beautiful

As I went walking one day
I decided to look for
what was beautiful

There was yellow rose
soft as velvet, brilliant
as the setting sun
And that was beautiful

While searching through a tree
I herd and saw a robin
singing and ruffling his
brightly colored breast
And that was beautiful

Sitting by the side of a lake
a friendly dog came by
and we played for awhile
And that was beautiful

Walking on down the road
I came upon you
And you smiled and said hi
come and walk with me
And I said this is the
most beautiful of all that
I found beautiful

To Cry

If I should cry
who would join me

Would they ask
why I cry

If they laughed
at my tears

Would it be because
they know not how to cry

If I should cry
who would understand

That my time has come
and all that is left
is a time,
a time to cry

Wondering Soul

Is there not for a
forsaken soul
A chance to
become whole

For a soul that searches
a whole life through
A wondering soul
that passes through
you and me

And yearns to spend time
With a calmer soul

Does your soul
ever wander
from soul to soul?

Is there not for a
forsaken soul
A chance to become whole

For a soul in turmoil
a chance
to repose in the arms
of a calmer soul

A Week

I took a week to let
my mind wander
through you and through me

If I but knew you
what a marvelous time
we could have
with our minds

We could communicate with
our minds
Our touch would tell us
so much
of how our minds yearn
to touch

*Thoughts from
the Journey Through*

~Seasons~

Night Song

Upon a Christmas night
I heard a gentle voice
calling
Come share this night
with me

Share my glistening tree
built over my
Christmas crib

Catch the love beaming
from my eyes
Reflected by the
fire's glow

Among the brilliance
of the stars
I heard a gentle voice
calling
Come share my
Christmas night

I'll give to you the gifts
made by my hands
And you give to me
the gifts made
by yours

Come, sit and we shall
sing soft and low
And listent to
the night

In the cold crisp air
I heard a gentle voice
calling
Come share this night
with me

Cradle me in your arms
with love divine
And I will cradle you
in mine
And together we shall
hear
How love grows and
becomes divine

A child's voice calling
on a Christmas night
Ever so gentle
yet heard beyond the stars
Come share this night

For on a Christmas night
the world could
Never be closer to
love divine

This is the voice of my son, Kevin, speaking for all children.

Copper Moon of Autumn Dreams

Copper Moon of
Autumn Dreams

Years of dreams
of walking time

Takes you through
the corridors
of time

Dream back
dream back

Youth is a living
memory

First love not
forgotten

Chosen love still dear
to the heart

Dream back
dream back

Copper Moon of
Autumn Dreams

Child of wonderment
first beheld

Every Child walks
into the dream

Carrying on the
union of love

Copper Moon of
Autumn dreams

Takes you through
the corridors
of time

When there is
Just we two

To live and create
memories for
eternity

Years of dreams
of waking time

Take you through
the corridors
of time

And give full bloom
to
Copper moon of Autumn dreams

Aurora Borealis

Here do I stand
in peaceful silence

To watch my symphony
of silence

Aurora Borealis my
symphony in silence

Illuminate my night
in splendid silence

Enrapture me around
in your multicolored lights

Fill my eye to my
heart's delight

In silence, in silence
play your symphony

Tug me to your crescendos
Dance in my heart
'til I whirl in delight

Illuminate my night
in splendid silence

Settle me down in
your lullabies

and keep me
in peaceful silence

Aurora Borealis my
symphony in silence

Lamenting on Winter

The frozen days
the frozen nights
the frozen horse
Fill me with no
delight

Jack Frost has
ripped off my nose
bubbled my ears
and froze my toes

The plumbing has
gone awry
and once again the
back house has seen
my backside

Shivering and quaking
I wait
For the long nights
to wane
and the sun to warm
my days again

Thoughts from
the Journey Through

~Shiloh~

Shiloh

I must go to Shiloh
the walk would be
tremendous

Must I walk it
all alone

This trip to
distant Shiloh

Walk on, walk on
to Shiloh

What price the walk
to Shiloh

A price I am strong enough
to pay

Walk on, walk on
to Shiloh

Cannot someone take
my hand and say

I'll walk with you
to Shiloh
Walk on, walk on
to Shiloh

Do you know how far
it is to Shiloh

Is it the distance of an
outstretched hand

Or is it on the
highest mountain top

Walk on, walk on
to Shiloh

The summit is at hand
the distance isn't far now

Can one find peace
in Shiloh*

*I'll leave it to you to find Shiloh

Number 14

*(Steam engine restored by
Lake Superior Railroad Museum)*

I sit by a track,
an abandoned track,
to bring an old dream
from the past back

A long ago sound
almost forgotten
but for our dreams
sounds never forgotten

I listen in my dream,
a laboring sound
in my dream
a shrill whistle
shatters my dream
I hear a bell
not in my dream

Old Number 14
is laboring down the track
in all its glory
coming down the track

With good friends
in a like minded dream
we sing the songs of old
that come out of our dreams
for Old Number 14
has given life to our dream

*(I've volunteered at the museum for 20 years.
The hours of volunteering is repaid a
thousand times over in these moments of joy.)*

Seasons

There is no lovelier time of year
Than when the trees
have slipped their green
And become the colors
of your dreams
Glistening and gleaming
listening and deceiving
Is to the winter
we are betrothed
With every attempt at
ebbing out
With forceful ebbing
with triumphant budding
Is to spring that brings
forth love.

A Smile

I wonder if a lion smiles

When with a full stomach
the lion languishes
in the noon day sun

For the depth of a smile
is only known to them
who enjoy a good smile

And the depth of the lion's smile
depends on whether he ate the
poacher or the big game hunter

Oh, you say
What would be the difference?
Why, said the lion
with a broad smile,
The big game hunter
had more poundage

Bill's note:
I've taught creative writing in the St. Louis County Jail for six years. This is a letter from one of my students. It truly is one of the many rewards of volunteering. There is no money to equal this reward.

The Teacher
Dedicated 2 Bill
by Darrell Dalton

4 a long time I've truly wondered
what a teacher is:

For a poverty-stricken person
like myself, all I had for teachers
were street wiz:

I been told that teachers are the ones
that make you think about true self
and true self-worth:

Why have I been cursed with gift of Bill:

Well, Bill, I don't know
if you've ever been given
the teacher's award,
but I've put you in the all time
Teachers' Hall of Fame.

The Leader
Dedicated to Al Hunter

For he who takes up the
burden of others
Walks taller than the
tallest trees
Knows the lateness
of the moon
Views the sunrise
with open heart
Walks the path of the
ancestors
In search of the peaceful
answer

The burden to give
is the sharing of
inner wisdom
The constant search for
an answer to the simple
word, Why!
A constant trying of trying
to untie the "Gordian Knot"
Without harming the hemp

When it is time to lay
the burden down

May you pass the burden on
to one
Whose heart is as full
of wisdom
as yours

Then may the Great Spirit
wrap the wings of wisdom
around you and say

Bide with me forever in the
"Valley of Peace and Wisdom"

For you, Al, on your election to Chief of you Tribe
My Anam Cara,
Bill DeRoche

Prayer

Is a soul's draught prayer
to be left upon the wind
If ever to be heard
never to be seen
Or is it to be carried aloft
on wings given by
someone unknown

To be answered by that
someone yet unknown
Only by faith's bent knee
shall it ever take wings
To be carried to him
yet still unknown

Peace

Peace, quiet peace
Will man ever be at peace
Let each man come to know
his soul and find peace

Let us each come to know
that we are brothers in one
And to know that we must share
the resources of our soul
Peace written upon the Tablet
but not conceived in men's souls
Leaves the mind as swiftly as the wind

Come and walk the hallowed archives
of written peace
And you will know that peace
is not in men's souls
Let just once the written peace
burn into men's souls
And men will then know that
their souls are the tablet

*Written on the evening of the signing
of the peace treaty in Vietnam*

Parting

Parting with the aged
is a closing of a dream
Parting with a dream
is awakening to the ages
Parting with love
is first finding love
Parting to eternal peace
is first having been born
Parting with our love on earth
is finding love forever
Parting with out spirit
is the beginning to live forever
Parting is all that is
certain to the earth
Parting is finding that hope
is certain